DAYS OF CHANGE

C *Creative Education*

BY RACHAEL HANEL

Published by Creative Education
P.O. Box 227, Mankato, Minnesota 56002
Creative Education is an imprint of The Creative Company.

Cover design and art direction by Rita Marshall
Interior design and book production by The Design Lab
Printed in the United States of America

Photographs by Alamy (Nick Haslam, Lebrecht Music and
Arts Photo Library, Mary Evans Picture Library, North Wind
Picture Archives, Peter Arnold Inc., Pictorial Press, Visual Arts
Library), Corbis (Bettmann, Hulton-Deutsch Collection), Getty
Images (AFP, Hulton Archive, Time Life Pictures)

Library of Congress Cataloging-in-Publication Data
Hanel, Rachael.
The slave trade / by Rachael Hanel.
p. cm. – (Days of change)
Includes bibliographical references and index.
ISBN-13: 978-1-58341-550-4
1. Slave trade–History. 2. Slavery–History. 3. Slavery–
Philosophy. I. Title.
HT871.H36 2007
306.3'6209–dc22   2006020149

9 8 7 6 5 4 3 2

THE SLAVE TRADE

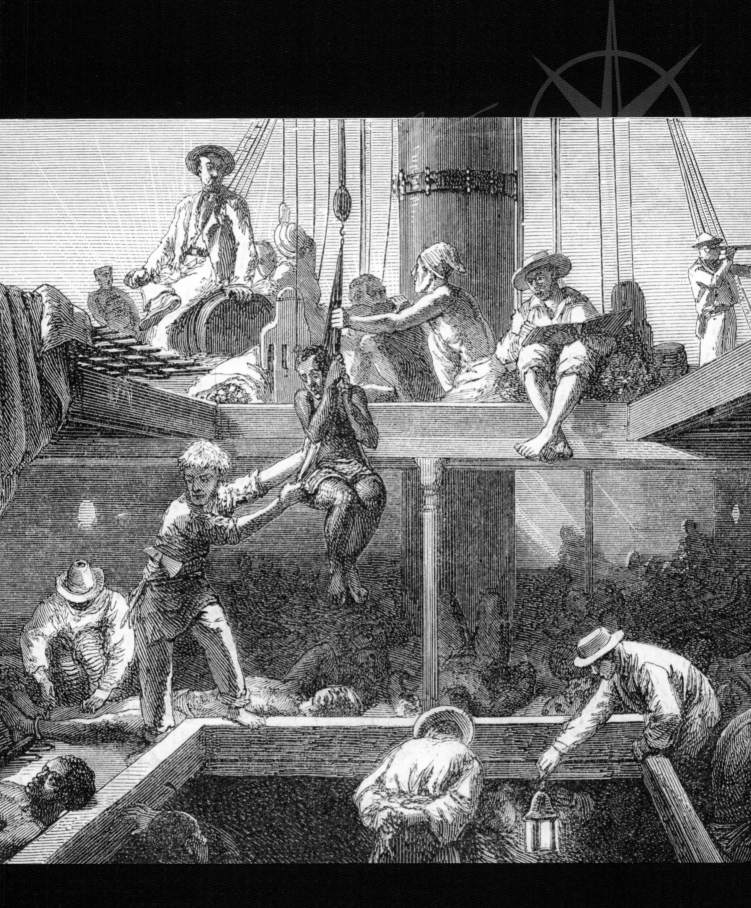

From the time they were captured and lowered into the cramped hold of a ship,
African slaves were treated more like animals than human beings.

The man's wide eyes surveyed the ship's dark,

damp hold. He saw his fellow villagers, who just weeks before had farmed, hunted, and danced in their African homeland. Now they were shackled to each other like animals. Each claimed just a few square feet of wiggle room—not that they could move much with their wrists and legs chained. The man was humiliated; often, he could not reach the bucket meant for human waste. Screams and moans filled the rank air during the weeks-long voyage across the roiling Atlantic Ocean. For those Africans who survived this harrowing journey, their lives in a new world—the Americas—would not improve. There, they would be slaves.

For 400 years, from the mid-1400s to the late 1800s, slavers forced as many as 15 million Africans from their homes and transported them across the ocean. Traders from countries such as Portugal, the Netherlands, and Britain were mostly responsible for this vast slave trade. It wasn't until the 19th century that increasingly loud questions about the morality of selling human life helped bring the trade to a halt. Still, the effects that centuries of subjugation had upon Africans, as well as debates about atonement for this awful time in history, would long linger.

5

6

Before the transatlantic slave trade started in the 1440s, Europe, Asia, and Africa started to break out of their cultural, geographic, and political isolation. A bustling land trade commenced throughout Europe, northern Africa, the Middle East, and Asia. European adventurers such as Italian Marco Polo traveled to China and Mongolia, and Christian missionaries also trekked eastward, seeking converts. The exchange of goods and ideas connected different cultures. Middle Eastern architecture influenced building styles in Europe and India, while spices from Asia—such as cinnamon, nutmeg, and cloves—influenced European cooking. Gold mined in Africa became a valued commodity throughout the Eastern Hemisphere. The first strings of a web that would soon connect the globe had been cast.

A GLOBAL NETWORK

In the Middle Ages leading up to the 15th century, Africa was its own thriving continent. Instead of formal country borders, tribal barriers divided the continent, and rich and powerful kings ruled hundreds of different regions. North African Muslim traders dominated intercontinental routes of commerce and traded salt, ivory, and wood to Europeans and Asians.

The Americas were also home to various indigenous peoples at this time, tribes who lived in relative isolation but sometimes crossed paths with one another in ways that were both peaceful and violent. North American tribes such as the Iroquois and Navajo did not have sophisticated trade routes and cities like those found across the ocean. However, in Central and South

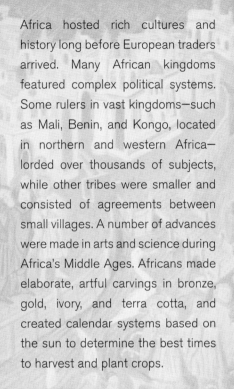

Africa hosted rich cultures and history long before European traders arrived. Many African kingdoms featured complex political systems. Some rulers in vast kingdoms—such as Mali, Benin, and Kongo, located in northern and western Africa—lorded over thousands of subjects, while other tribes were smaller and consisted of agreements between small villages. A number of advances were made in arts and science during Africa's Middle Ages. Africans made elaborate, artful carvings in bronze, gold, ivory, and terra cotta, and created calendar systems based on the sun to determine the best times to harvest and plant crops.

While much of Europe's trade revolved around the rich city of Venice, Italy (above), land trade routes also crisscrossed Africa, connecting many of the continent's kingdoms.

America, native peoples such as the Mayans, Aztecs, and Incas created thriving cities, stunning architecture, and complex political networks complete with emperors and clear class distinctions.

In Europe, most territory fell under the rule of kings and princes. The time period immediately preceding the Atlantic slave trade is considered a golden age of European history. Literature, philosophy, and theater flourished. Painters such as the Italian Giotto and writers such as Englishman Geoffrey Chaucer influenced thought and culture through their works, and the Catholic Church served as a pillar of guidance in most communities. The upper class, made rich through trade, embraced prosperity, while the lower classes worked in ways that served the rich—in banking and the selling of goods, for example. By the 15th century, the constant quest for more wealth led Europeans to turn their eyes to new horizons. People had long looked upon the vast ocean and asked, "What lies beyond?" But now, finally, technology was advancing enough to allow exploration of the sea and distant lands. Ships became stronger and sturdier, and new seafaring instruments such as the compass and astrolabe allowed for navigation using stars and the sun.

"You may make my grave wherever you will
In a lowly vale or a lofty hill
You may make it among earth's humblest graves,
But not in a land where men are slaves."

FRANCES ELLEN WATKINS (HARPER),
a free black poet, in "Bury Me in a Free Land," 1858

8

Around the same time that the compass was invented, mapmaking capabilities improved, making sailing safer and enabling sailors to venture across larger bodies of water.

Prince Henry the Navigator of Portugal sponsored numerous expeditions to Africa, where he encouraged Portuguese settlers to colonize many of the lands they discovered.

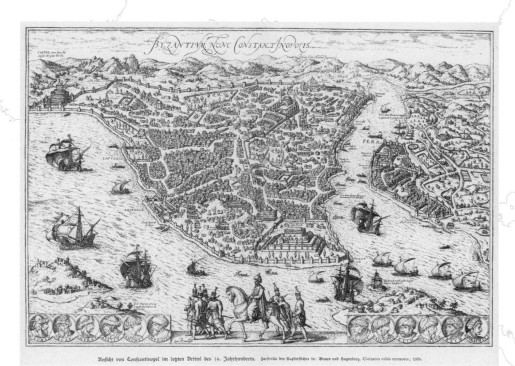

Ansicht von Constantinopel im letzten Drittel des 16. Jahrhunderts. Facsimile des Kupferstiches in: Braun und Hogenberg. Civitates orbis terrarum; 1576.

The Portuguese were the first Europeans to launch major sea expeditions in an era that became known as the Age of Discovery. Blocked from overland trade in the Middle East by the Ottoman Empire at the time, the Portuguese sought new routes to Asia. They traveled down the coast of Africa, rounded what is now South Africa, and journeyed on through the Indian Ocean to Asia. The famous Portuguese monarch Prince Henry the Navigator sent out expedition after expedition starting around the 1420s under the charge of explorers such as Bartolomeu Dias and Vasco da Gama. The Portuguese first sailed to Africa in the 1430s, most interested in reports of vast quantities of gold, and began exchanging goods with Muslim traders. The Portuguese left Europe with horses, cloth, wine, and guns, and sailed home with gold, ivory, and pepper.

During the Age of Discovery, the Ottoman Empire, which stood between Europe and the East, was a force to be reckoned with, quickly taking over new lands.

In Africa, the Portuguese noted that Africans traded not only goods but also humans. Muslims, Jews, and Africans had traded slaves for goods for centuries. The slavers forced millions of Africans—many of whom had lived as hunters and gatherers—from their homes in central, western, and eastern Africa, marching them across the hot desert on foot to northern Africa. About one in four slaves died during this arduous journey, and the surviving slaves were dispersed to lands such as Egypt and Morocco. Others crossed the Red Sea to Arabia or the Indian Ocean to Asia.

Some Portuguese explorers, such as Gaspar Corte-Real, ventured beyond Africa, crossing the Atlantic

Spanish explorer Juan Ponce de Leon

Ocean to what they called "The New World." Explorers of other nationalities soon followed, and the race was on to see which country could stake a claim to the most land. Italian explorers, most famously Christopher Columbus, sailed across the Atlantic to the islands of the Caribbean. French explorers such as Jacques Cartier traveled to North America. Spanish explorers Francisco Coronado and Hernán Cortés explored South America, while Juan Ponce de Leon went to Florida looking for a "fountain of youth."

The wide, varied landscapes of the Americas impressed Europeans, as did the availability of raw materials such as wood and precious metals. The explorers saw the potential

Spanish explorer Hernán Cortés's party landed in Mexico in 1519 and by 1521 had conquered the Aztec capital, Tenochtitlan, on the ruins of which was built Mexico City.

"The slave trade is the ruling principle of my people. It is the source and the glory of their wealth. . . . [T]he mother lulls the child to sleep with notes of triumph over an enemy reduced to slavery. . . ."

AFRICAN KING GEZO OF DAHOMEY, 1840

for agriculture and mining, and with it, the possibility of great wealth. But to work the land, the Europeans needed a large labor force. Europeans themselves were unaccustomed to the tropical climate found in much of the Americas and often fell ill from disease in the new land. They enslaved the native American populations when possible, but millions died from diseases—such as smallpox—that had been brought across the Atlantic. Europeans soon looked to Africa's existing slave trade. It seemed a promising solution, as Africans already lived in tropical climates, and many worked their own land as farmers and laborers.

Competition among the nations of Europe would soon ignite a bustling slave trade, as Portugal, Spain, France, and Britain all dedicated themselves to reaping the most money, power, and privilege in the Americas. Booming New World industries, such as sugar cultivation, needed a large supply of labor to be profitable. Europeans harvested sugar on islands in the Atlantic Ocean and, at first, used native islanders and Europeans (indentured servants, prisoners, and orphans) to work the land. But the need for more labor in the vast Americas was great.

Long-held cultural ideas gave most Europeans, accustomed to wide-ranging class distinctions, no qualms about trading other human beings and subjecting them to slavery.

Although there were slaves within Africa's borders, most of the Africans forced to toil in the fields of the Americas for white masters had not served as slaves in their homeland.

The countries of Europe were rich, and with this wealth came divisions in social classes. Rich Europeans looked down upon the poor, even in their own lands. For centuries, Europe was characterized by a feudal system, with kings and lords at the top and slave-like servants at the bottom. These servants, called serfs, toiled for little or no wage and were restricted in their movements, although some were able to buy their freedom after years of service.

Religion and skin color also played key roles in enabling slavery. European Christians viewed their religion as "civilized" and saw other religions as inferior. Because Africans were not Christian, traders believed they could morally be enslaved and forced to work. Some slave traders even convinced themselves they were giving Africans a better life in the Americas because they would there have a chance for baptism and, therefore, salvation. Further encouraging the human trade was many Europeans' unflinching belief in the righteousness and superiority of the white race. Until the 15th century's Age of Discovery opened up new lands, many white people had never seen a dark-skinned person. This difference in color allowed slave trading nations to see Africans as less than human and therefore property that could be bought and sold like farm animals.

"In this wretched hovel, all colors, except white—the only guilty one—both sexes, and all ages, are confined, exposed indiscriminately to all the contamination which may be expected in such society and under such seclusion. The inmates of . . . this class . . . are even worse treated; some of them, if my informants are to be believed, having been actually frozen to death, during the inclement winters which often prevail in the country."

E.S. ABDY, British visitor to Washington, D.C., describing a slave holding area in 1835

Slavery was already an old idea when Europeans began seeking African slaves; more than 2,500 years before, the Israelites had been enslaved in Egypt.

São Tomé is a small island off of Africa's west coast. The island was discovered by the Portuguese in 1472 and by the 16th century flourished as the slave trade grew. The island was an important trading post in the movement of slaves from southwest Africa to the Gold Coast, north of São Tomé. The Portuguese took Africans from the Kongo region in the south and exported them to traders on the Gold Coast. Throughout the 16th century, São Tomé remained a crucial stopping point in the slave trade from Africa to the Spanish Caribbean. Today, it is a small country along with the island of Principe and is a popular tourist destination.

The majority of the Africans captured and sold as part of the Atlantic slave trade were adult men, who outnumbered women captives two to one.

The Atlantic slave trade started slowly. In 1441, Portuguese slavers shipped 10 African slaves from the coast of Mauritania to Portugal, and three years later shipped home another 240 slaves. In 1502, the first African slaves to reach the New World arrived on the island of Hispaniola (modern-day Haiti and the Dominican Republic). Having secured their labor source, Europeans could now increase the amount of goods such as sugar, gold, and silver flowing out of the New World and use these items to engage in more trade in Africa to obtain more slaves. It was a cycle that would continue for more than 400 years.

"The economic ties between Asia, Europe, Africa, and America clearly involved a web of relationships that spans the globe. At the heart of this system was a Europe committed to consuming American plantation crops at an ever expanding rate. . . . Until European immigrants replaced them in the late 19th century, it was African slaves who enabled this consumption revolution to occur. Without that labor, most of America would never have developed at the pace it did."

HERBERT KLEIN, American historian, 1999

19

European slavers established a number of forts and outposts on the African coast and coastal islands, from which they traded with African merchants and leaders.

In the Atlantic slave trade, slavers transported Africans across the ocean to the Americas as part of a large triangular trade route. The first leg of the journey went from Europe to Africa and concluded with the trade of European goods for slaves. The second leg, commonly referred to as the Middle Passage, brought slaves across the Atlantic Ocean to the Americas. The final leg brought slave-produced goods—including sugar, cotton, tobacco, and precious metals—back to Europe.

THE HUMAN TRADE

The first part of the journey, from Europe to Africa's west coast, could take several months. First, a slave ship's captain needed enough men to work the ship. Since sailing was a demanding job with high mortality rates, it was sometimes difficult just finding a crew. Ships were often manned by desperate men who took the job as a last option. Sometimes men were even kidnapped and forced to join the crew, or were lured aboard a ship while drunk. Once a ship had its crew, preparation for the long trip took weeks, as the ship had to be packed with large volumes of food, as well as goods to trade. The actual journey during each of the three legs could take anywhere from weeks to months, depending on the wind. When the wind refused to fill a ship's sails, the vessel was left stationary at sea, often under a brutally hot sun in tropical areas. A ship's arrival could be delayed for weeks or months, and food and fresh water frequently ran low.

When a ship finally reached the west coast of Africa, it docked in a harbor for as long as several months

Nearly half of all slaves came from the interior of west-central Africa, including Angola and the region between the Congo River and present-day Cameroon. African rulers and those working for them brought the slaves to the coast to trade them to Europeans. Slave ships disembarked from all along the West African coast. The largest exporting regions were the Bight of Benin and Bight of Biafra ("bight" refers to a place along a coastline where the geography curves). The Bight of Benin was known as "The Slave Coast." Slaves also left from Senegambia, Sierra Leone, and southeastern Africa.

As the slave trade gathered force, slave ships regularly sailed in and out of African ports; by the 1780s, an average of 80,000 slaves a year were being shipped to the Americas.

while the Europeans traded with African kings. African rulers—such as Osei Tutu of the Ashanti kingdom (present-day Ghana) and Dogbari of Dahomey (present-day southern Benin)—became rich and powerful by trading Africans to white slavers. Europeans usually stayed on the coast and paid Africans in the form of iron, guns, and cloth to venture into the mainland's interior and come back with people to be shipped to the Americas. Africans almost always did the actual capturing of slaves, as they knew the continent's imposing interior better than Europeans.

Captured Africans' march to the coast and the waiting ships some-times was as long as 1,000 miles (1,600 km). The slaves might then wait weeks or months before actu-ally boarding a ship. During the wait, traders held slaves captive at the coast, often in prison-like holding

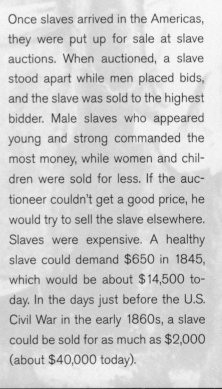

Once slaves arrived in the Americas, they were put up for sale at slave auctions. When auctioned, a slave stood apart while men placed bids, and the slave was sold to the highest bidder. Male slaves who appeared young and strong commanded the most money, while women and children were sold for less. If the auctioneer couldn't get a good price, he would try to sell the slave elsewhere. Slaves were expensive. A healthy slave could demand $650 in 1845, which would be about $14,500 today. In the days just before the U.S. Civil War in the early 1860s, a slave could be sold for as much as $2,000 (about $40,000 today).

African soldiers (second from left) stood guard over captured slaves; the slaves were then examined by European slavers, who negotiated their price with African traders.

As they awaited transport across the Atlantic, captured slaves were chained together in close quarters (top); aboard slave ships (bottom), conditions were even tighter.

pens. This time on the coast proved frightening for Africans in many ways. Already having been forced from their homes, families, and way of life, they now encountered white men for the first time, with their pale eyes, full beards, strange language, and unknown intentions. Slaves then suffered an unpleasant introduction to the ocean when they were forced onto small boats that ferried them to the large ships. These boats were prone to capsizing in rough waters, and slaves frequently drowned. Some slaves, realizing their bleak futures, committed suicide by refusing to eat while in holding pens or by jumping overboard from ships.

For those who boarded the ships, the journey across the Middle Passage was horrifying. Crews kept slaves below deck in dark, close, and filthy quarters. Large ships held about 500 slaves, while smaller ships transported about 100. Toward the end of the slave trade, in the early to mid-1800s, a few very large ships held upwards of 1,000 slaves. Disease often ran rampant; dysentery, a type of diarrhea, was common, as were respiratory illnesses. Some slaves died in

25

"The morning in which my town, Osogun, [was taken], . . . we were preparing breakfast without any apprehension when . . . a rumor was spread in the town that the enemies had approached. . . . [W]omen, some with three, four, or six children clinging to their arms, with the infants on their backs and such baggage as they could carry on their heads, [ran] as fast as they could through the prickly shrubs . . . [but] were overtaken and caught . . . with a noose of rope thrown over the neck of every individual, to be led in the manner of goats tied together, under the drove of one man. In many cases a family was violently divided between three or four enemies, who each led his away to see one another no more."

SAMUEL AJAYI CROWTHER, a captured slave from Nigeria, 1837

rebellion attempts against the ship's crew. Despite the odds against them, many tried to revolt. It is estimated that one out of every 10 ships experienced a slave uprising. Other dangers encountered along the Middle Passage included bad weather and pirate attacks.

As cruelly as slaves were housed, it was in the best interest of a ship's crew to protect the health of their slaves, since there was more money to be made if a ship came into port with strong slaves ready to work. Men and women were housed in separate quarters. Female slaves and children were sometimes afforded limited freedom, as women often performed duties for the crew such as cooking or providing medical care. Other slaves served as interpreters. On some ships, slaves were allowed on deck for fresh air and limited exercise. A ship's human cargo was usually provided two or three meals of beans, rice, or corn a day, provided the food didn't spoil or become scarce on the long voyage.

Researchers well-versed in the Atlantic slave trade estimate that between 12 million and 15 million Africans were shipped across the ocean over the course of 400 years. An estimated 26,000 slaving voyages took place, and three out

"The slaves were all enclosed under grated hatchways between decks. The space was so low that they sat between each other's legs and [were] stowed so close together that there was no possibility of their lying down or at all changing their position by night or day. As they belonged to and were shipped on account of different individuals, they were all branded like sheep with the owner's marks of different forms."

REVEREND ROBERT WALSH, upon inspecting a seized slave ship, May 22, 1829

26

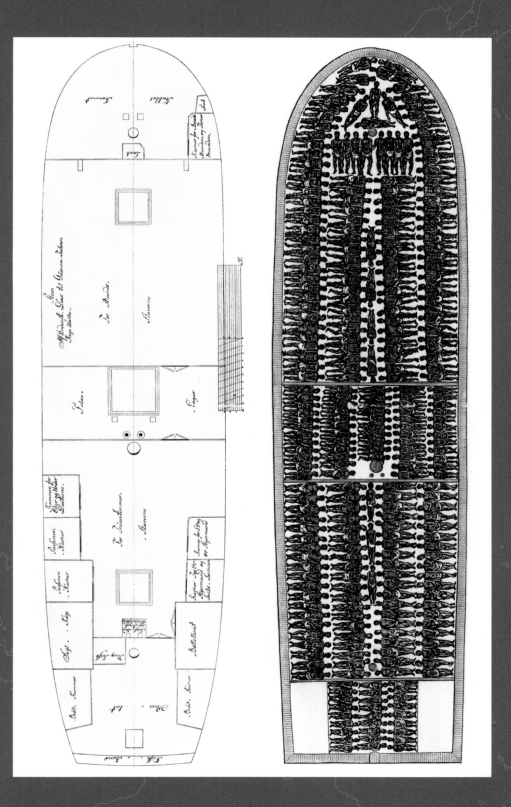

The deck plan of a slave ship reveals how closely slaves were packed—often on decks only five feet (1.5 m) high—on a journey that could take from one to two months.

"*The closeness of the place, and the heat of the climate, added to the number in the ship, which was so crowded that each had scarcely room to turn himself, almost suffocated us. This produced copious perspirations, so that the air soon became unfit for respiration, from a variety of loathsome smells, and brought on a sickness among the slaves, of which many died.*"

OLAUDAH EQUIANO, author and former slave, 1789

of every four slaves were shipped on either a Portuguese or British ship. The exact number of slave deaths that occurred during the Middle Passage is difficult to determine. Even though slaving ship captains usually kept good records of mortality on account of the value of their cargo, only about one-fifth of all ships' records exist today. Based on that information, it has been estimated that 12 percent of all slaves who boarded a ship in Africa died during the ocean crossing.

Once slaves reached the Americas, their hardships took a new form. Back on land, they were again herded into holding cells. Then, it was time for the sale. Potential buyers physically examined slaves, often in humiliating ways, and new owners frequently branded their new slaves with hot irons to mark them as property. If an African family managed to stay together through the ocean journey, it was here in the Americas that husbands and wives, parents and children, and brothers and sisters were split up among different owners, never to see each other again.

After the coastal sale, another journey awaited the slaves. Often, this journey to their new home was by land, but some slaves had to board yet another ship. Once at their destination, slaves faced a life of hard labor with almost no chance for freedom. Many slaves worked to extract gold and silver from mines in Central and South America, while North

29

Slaves who survived the journey across the Atlantic were auctioned off to eager buyers; in the later years of the slave trade, the prices for slaves rose to an all-time high.

Many slaves in Mexico and South American countries such as Brazil preferred working in silver mines over plantation work. Slave miners were allowed more freedom than their field counterparts and were sometimes rewarded with brandy and tobacco. If they met a certain quota of silver in a day, their owners might even allow them to keep extra mined silver for themselves, and some slaves were able to cash in their collected silver and buy freedom. The work was far from ideal, however; in mines, they were subjected to dangerous cave-ins, floods, and fires. The average working life of a miner was only six to eight years.

Although slaves in Brazil preferred working in mines, many of the country's slaves labored on sugarcane plantations, some processing the cane in sugar mills.

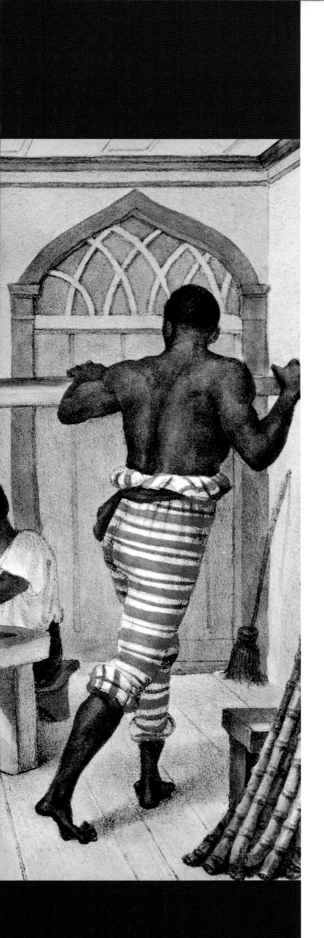

American slaves worked mainly on large agricultural plantations, cultivating and harvesting cotton, sugar, and tobacco. The journey inland might not even be their last, as slaves were routinely sold from one owner to another.

In the Americas, slaves were distributed to many different areas. The most common destination was Brazil, which received 41 percent of slaves in the Atlantic trade. Brazil imported slaves during most of the four centuries of the Atlantic slave trade, whereas places such as the United States barred the importation of new slaves decades before the slave trade officially ended. Slaves going to the British colonies, which later became the U.S., accounted for fewer than four percent of all slaves crossing the ocean.

By the 18th and 19th centuries, attitudes toward slavery started to change. This change in thinking can be traced to the "Age of Enlightenment" that marked Europe during this time. New philosophers such as Voltaire of France and David Hume of Scotland rose to prominence and promoted the notion of equality. For the first time, the "right" to own other human beings was publicly questioned. Religion also factored into the change of thought. New religions, such as the Society of Friends (commonly known as the Quakers), embraced compassion for all humans; as soon as the late 1700s and early 1800s, American Quakers were encouraged to free their slaves, and many did. As the years went by, more people throughout the U.S. and Europe took up the abolitionist cause, seeking to put an end to the human trade. The British abolished the slave trade in 1807, while the U.S. halted the importation of slaves in 1808. The last recorded transport of slaves in the Atlantic trade arrived in Cuba in 1867. By 1865, slavery itself was abolished in the U.S. Brazil was the last country to abolish the practice, doing so in 1888. The selling of human lives had officially come to an end.

"There is a . . . dreadful effect of this trade upon the minds of those who are engaged in it. . . . I know of no method of getting money . . . which has so direct a tendency to efface the moral sense, to rob the heart of every gentle and humane disposition and to harden it like steel, against all impressions of sensibility."

JOHN NEWTON, a slave trader turned abolitionist, 1788

32

In 1839, the slave schooner *Amistad* was headed to Cuba with 49 Africans when the slaves seized upon a chance for revolt behind a leader named Cinque, who broke free of his chains and led a rebellion that killed most of the ship's crew. The slaves tried to steer the ship to Africa, but it ended up in U.S. waters, where it was captured and the Africans arrested. Abolitionists used the *Amistad* to plead their case against slavery, and a trial ensued that reached the U.S. Supreme Court in 1841. The court found in favor of the would-be slaves and set them free, and the 35 Africans who had survived the long ordeal returned to Africa.

More than 160 years after the *Amistad* rebellion, in March 2000, a replica of the *Amistad* was launched from Connecticut, with the mission of educating people about slavery.

34

Although the slave trade ended nearly 200 years ago, the effects of this enormous injustice can still be seen in all parts of the world, and many still cause hot debate. The trade not only exported humans out of Africa but also brought to Africa many European goods. Even after the Atlantic slave trade ended, some African rulers—such as King Gezo of Dahomey—continued to find wealth through the human trade. Some scholars, including Ghanaian Adu Boahen, have argued that because African leaders focused so intently on the human trade, they never developed the lucrative manufacturing industries found in North America and Europe, leaving Africa a continent of mostly poor, third-world countries today.

Yet while some historians main-tain that the loss of as many as 15 million people devastated Africa's cultural landscape, creative capa-bilities, and technological capabili-ties, others say the effects weren't that dramatic because the exodus occurred over four centuries and the population that stayed in Africa reproduced sufficiently to make up for those losses. In fact, the African popula-tion did not seem to lose numbers during the slave trade. Ironically, the import of new and better foods supplied by slave labor in the Americas improved the diet and health of Africans in some areas of the continent.

A LINGERING LEGACY

While Africa's demographics did not change greatly, the popu-lation in the New World became increasingly diverse as a result of

Once in the U.S, many slaves tried to escape from their owners. One popular route to freedom, known as the Underground Railroad, led from slave states in the South to free states in the North. The Underground Railroad, given that symbolic name in 1831 by those who took the path, was not really a railroad; instead, it was a route peppered with "safe houses" where slaves could rest and hide. Harriet Tubman, a former slave, is estimated to have ushered around 300 slaves to freedom on this route, making many risky returns into the South to help others.

During the U.S. Civil War (1861–65), which was fought in part over the issue of slavery, the Navy employed thousands of freed slaves; after the war, all slaves were freed.

Because the slave trade occurred so long ago, complete and accurate records are hard to find. As a result, historians and researchers find it difficult to agree on the precise numbers of Africans who were taken across the ocean and sold into slavery. Only in the 1960s did researchers start to professionally analyze data, using what ship logs and business records existed, to form fact-based estimates. While 12 to 15 million is the most widely accepted total for slaves taken out of Africa, some estimates from the days of abolition ranged as high as 28 million.

Although many records from slave ships have been destroyed, those that exist, such as this Spanish document, include detailed information about their human cargo.

the slave trade. By 1850, Africans or descendants of Africans accounted for 20 percent of the New World population. The African population was even higher in places such as the Caribbean islands, where the tropical weather contributed to a high mortality rate, and where new slaves were therefore imported in high numbers. Today, descendants of slaves live in all parts of the Western Hemisphere. While relatively few slaves were imported to the U.S., their low death rates (due in part to a more moderate climate) and high birth rates combined for a population explosion. By 1825, slaves in the U.S. accounted for one-third of all slaves in the Americas, with most of those slaves having been born in the U.S.

The merging of cultures in the Americas combined to create a number of new traditions in places where slave populations existed. When slavers brought Africans to the Americas, the slaves brought their traditions and rituals with them. For many, keeping certain traditions helped remind them of home, for they knew they would never return. Many slaves maintained their styles of dance, dress, and food preparation. Many African cultures were adept at

"As a Southerner, I feel that it is my duty to stand up here tonight and bear testimony against slavery. I have seen it—I have seen it. I know it has horrors that can never be described. I was brought up under its wing: I witnessed for many years its demoralizing influences, and its destructiveness to human happiness. It is admitted by some that the slave is not happy under the worst forms of slavery. But I have never seen a happy slave."

ANGELINA GRIMKE WELD,
American abolitionist, 1838

37

skills such as basket-weaving, and slaves brought these abilities to the New World as well. Modern forms of music such as jazz, blues, and rock can be traced back to the rhythmic beats that Africans brought with them. Languages also combined; for example, the Gullah dialect found in coastal South Carolina today retains an African vocabulary.

Many descendants of Africans continue rich storytelling traditions, often in the form of oral histories. In 1976, African American author Alex Haley fictionalized the slave stories his family had passed down through the centuries in his best-selling book *Roots*. The next year, the book was made into an ABC television miniseries viewed by millions of Americans, making it one of the most successful shows of all time. The book and screen adaptation helped many Americans to confront

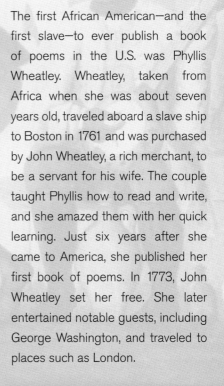

The first African American—and the first slave—to ever publish a book of poems in the U.S. was Phyllis Wheatley. Wheatley, taken from Africa when she was about seven years old, traveled aboard a slave ship to Boston in 1761 and was purchased by John Wheatley, a rich merchant, to be a servant for his wife. The couple taught Phyllis how to read and write, and she amazed them with her quick learning. Just six years after she came to America, she published her first book of poems. In 1773, John Wheatley set her free. She later entertained notable guests, including George Washington, and traveled to places such as London.

Combining their own customs with those of their white masters, many slaves held festive weddings, some outdoors and some inside the plantation house.

Many slaves, including the fictional Tom (center) from Harriet Beecher Stowe's novel *Uncle Tom's Cabin* were Christian; the few who were literate often read from the Bible.

the ugly history and realities of the slave trade and subsequent slavery, and also inspired other African Americans to begin similar quests to learn their family stories.

For all their trials and tribulations, slaves showed remarkable fortitude. Faced with a new land and new language, and—in many cases—torn apart from their biological families, they created new communities. Even if slaves were not related by blood, they were united in the fact that they all shared the same circumstances, and they forged strong bonds in their shared misery. Many slaves embraced Christianity and came to identify with tales of biblical suffering, such as that of Moses, Job, and Jesus. Slaves created spiritual songs, often based on an African call-and-response style. These spirituals live on and remain an important cornerstone of many churches today. Yet other Africans retained their religion. Voodoo, which is still practiced in some parts of the southern U.S. and the Caribbean islands, is an African religion that survived the ocean crossing.

The majority of slaves in the Americas saw little change during their lifetimes. Over the course of four centuries, millions were born into slavery and died in slavery. They practiced the same routines of hard physical labor in fields and mines day after day. New slaves brought directly from Africa experienced the trauma of being ripped from their homeland

41

Civil rights leader Martin Luther King Jr.

and families and taken to a foreign place. Those experiences and memories of home stayed with them always. Only those who were alive when slavery was abolished (from 1834 to 1838 in the British colonies, and 1865 in the U.S.) saw any type of positive change. Having been regarded as property their whole lives, they were now suddenly free to move wherever they pleased.

Yet even when slaves were granted freedom, they faced racism and harsh oppression, especially in the U.S. After slavery ended, negative stereotyping based on African Americans' physical characteristics—such as hair texture and facial features—became common, and many whites refused to accept them as equals. Laws that enforced segregation in the U.S., known as Jim Crow laws, dictated that blacks couldn't eat in the same restaurants as whites, drink from the same water fountains, or use the same public restrooms. The civil rights movement that ultimately undid this segregation gained steam in 1955 when a black seamstress named Rosa Parks refused to yield her seat in the front of a Montgomery, Alabama, city bus to a white passenger. Although African American leaders such as Martin Luther King Jr. did much to promote equality among all races, deep-rooted racial tensions and divisions remain today.

In 1965, Martin Luther King Jr. led a civil rights march in Alabama to protest against voter qualification tests, which kept many Southern blacks from voting.

Today, some countries, such as Great Britain, publicly debate whether their governments should formally apologize for the slave trade. European countries that were once world superpowers—namely, Britain, Portugal, Spain, and France—in particular search for answers, since Europeans played such an integral role in the human cargo commerce. Discussion also continues as to whether some form of payment, called reparations, should be made to African Americans for the injustice suffered by their ancestors. But the issue of reparations is a difficult one rife with questions. Who would make the payments? Who would receive payments? Can reparations be given for an activity that was once legal? How much money would be distributed? Some have suggested it would take many billions of dollars to help atone for the atrocities Africans experienced as slaves.

"Until we as a society fully reckon with the history of slavery in all its dimensions . . . and overcome our historical denial of the central shaping role that slavery has played in the creating of all of America's social, political, cultural, and economic institutions, we cannot truly begin to confront the so-called race problem in this country."

HENRY LOUIS GATES, African American scholar, January 2001

Although the Atlantic slave trade died long ago, different types of slave trading continue around the world. In Pakistan, Niger, Haiti, and other places across the globe, many people are forced to work in fields and factories under threat of violence to themselves or their loved ones. The United Nations estimates that 20 million people—men, women, and

44

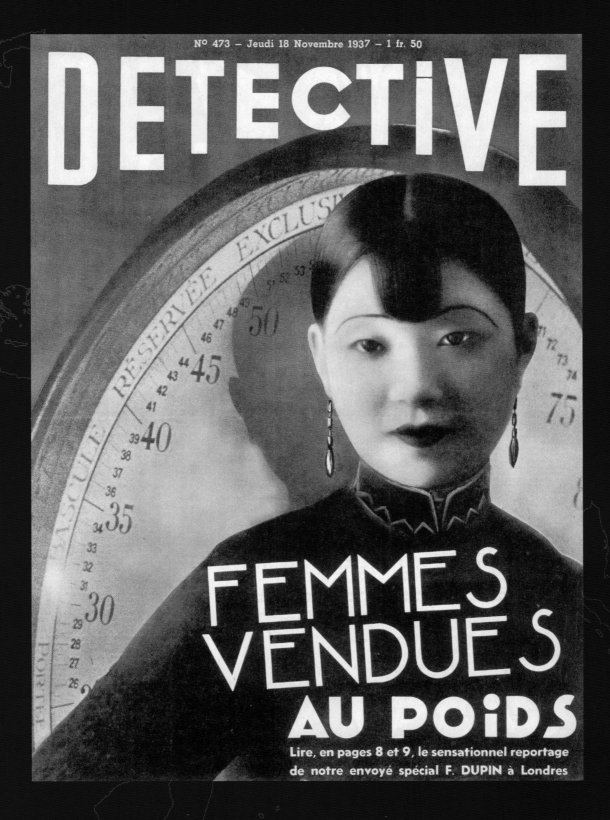

N° 473 — Jeudi 18 Novembre 1937 — 1 fr. 50

DETECTIVE

FEMMES VENDUES AU POIDS

Lire, en pages 8 et 9, le sensationnel reportage de notre envoyé spécial F. DUPIN à Londres

In the mid-1930s, a French-language magazine reported that Chinese girls were being sold—at prices based on their weight—in London, a new form of the slave trade.

In 1972, divers made a discovery that revealed firsthand what a slave ship looked like. Off the coast of Florida, they found the wreck of the British ship *Henrietta Marie*. In the spring of 1700, the *Henrietta Marie* took 206 Africans to the island of Jamaica. On its return journey to England, the ship was loaded with goods such as indigo, cotton, and sugar, but sank early into its voyage. Items from the wreck—including iron shackles—are today displayed at the Mel Fisher Maritime Heritage Society in Key West, Florida, and have helped researchers recreate life aboard a slave ship.

Although slave ships no longer traverse the rough waters of the Atlantic Ocean, slavery's lasting effects—and its modern forms—still haunt the world.

children—are enslaved worldwide. In the U.S., an estimated 20,000 people are trafficked in every year from poor nations of the world and compelled to work under slave-like conditions on farms, in factories, or as prostitutes.

Although huge ships no longer carry human cargo across the turbulent waves of the Atlantic Ocean, the transatlantic slave trade will always be remembered as one of the most shameful chapters in the world's history. The ghosts of slaves who died in ship holds or worked in the fields, plantation houses, and mines of the Americas still linger today. Their stories, passed down from generation to generation, provide an opportunity to learn from misdeeds of the past—and express a hope for a world one day entirely free from human bondage.

BIBLIOGRAPHY

Eltis, David. *The Rise of African Slavery in the Americas.*
New York: Cambridge University Press, 1999.

Hatt, Christine. *The African-American Slave Trade.*
North Mankato, Minn.: Smart Apple Media, 2003.

Klein, Herbert S. *The Atlantic Slave Trade.*
New York: Cambridge University Press, 1999.

Northrup, David, ed. *The Atlantic Slave Trade.*
Boston: Houghton Mifflin Company, 2002.

Postma, Johannes. *The Atlantic Slave Trade.*
Westport, Conn.: Greenwood Press, 2003.

Thomas, Hugh. *The Slave Trade: The Story of the Atlantic Slave Trade: 1440–1870.* New York: Simon and Schuster, 1997.

INDEX

abolition 32, 33, 36, 37, 42
Africa 5, 6, 7, 11, 12, 14, 15, 18, 19, 20, 21, 22, 25, 29, 33, 34, 36, 37, 38, 41
Age of Discovery 11, 16
Age of Enlightenment 32
Americas 5, 6, 8, 12, 15, 16, 19, 20, 22, 29, 30, 31, 34, 37, 41, 47
Amistad 33
Asia 6, 11, 12, 19
Atlantic Ocean 5, 6, 8, 12, 15, 19, 20, 25, 26, 29, 31, 32, 36, 41, 47
Brazil 30, 31, 32
Britain 5, 8, 15, 16, 29, 32, 42, 44, 46
Caribbean islands 12, 18, 19, 32, 33, 37, 41, 46
Cartier, Jacques 12
civil rights movement 42
Columbus, Christopher 12
Coronado, Francisco 12
Corte-Real, Gaspar 12
Cortés, Hernán 12
da Gama, Vasco 11
de Leon, Juan Ponce 12
Dias, Bartolomeu 11
Europe 6, 8, 11, 15, 16, 19, 20, 32, 34, 44
France 12, 15, 32, 44
Haley, Alex 38
    Roots 38
Henry the Navigator, Prince of Portugal 11

King, Martin Luther Jr. 42
Middle East 6, 11
Middle Passage 20, 25, 26, 29
mines 6, 15, 29, 30, 41, 47
Netherlands 5
Parks, Rosa 42
plantations 19, 30, 31, 41, 47
Polo, Marco 6
Portugal 5, 11, 12, 15, 18, 19, 29, 44
reparations 5, 44
segregation 42
slave ships 5, 20, 21, 22, 25, 26, 28, 29, 33, 36, 46, 47
slaves
    capture 5, 22, 25
    deaths 12, 16, 25, 28, 29, 37, 41, 47
    journey 5, 12, 18, 20, 22, 25, 26, 28, 29, 31
    revolts 26, 33
slave trade
    end of 5, 31, 32, 34
    modern 44, 47
    route 20
    within Africa 12, 15, 21, 22, 34
slave traders 5, 12, 16, 18, 19, 20, 22, 32, 37
Spain 12, 15, 44
United States 16, 31, 32, 33, 37, 38, 41, 42, 44, 46, 47